Quickbooks

A simple guide to Quickbooks for beginners, bookkeeping, and accounting basics

Table of Contents

Introduction 3

Chapter 1 What is Quickbooks and is it Right for Your Business? 4

Chapter 2 Different Versions of Quickbooks 6

Chapter 3 Five Basic Functions of Quickbooks 9

Chapter 4 Completing the Easy Step Interview 12

Chapter 5 Setting up your Chart of Accounts List 14

Chapter 6 Setting up the Item List 19

Chapter 7 Setting Up the Payroll Item List 24

Chapter 8 Setting up Your Customer List 26

Chapter 9 Setting up the Vendor and Employee Lists 29

Chapter 10 How to Invoice Your Customers 36

Chapter 11 Budgeting Within Quickbooks 40

Chapter 12 Using Quickbooks for Taxes 44

Chapter 13 How to Create Reports 48

Chapter 14 Quickbooks Add-Ons 50

Chapter 15 Quickbooks Shortcuts 55

Chapter 16 Quickbooks Troubleshooting 62

Chapter 17 Final Thoughts on Quickbooks 66

Conclusion 67

Introduction

Thank you for taking the time to pick up this book about Quickbooks!

This book covers the topic of Quickbooks and how to use it to manage the accounting of your own small business.

Quickbooks is the most popular accounting software available, and is relatively intuitive and simple to use once you understand its primary features! This book aims to teach you these features, and will guide you step by step through all of the functions you will regularly be using on Quickbooks.

At the completion of this book you will have a good understanding of the different Quickbooks features, and how to use them efficiently and effectively to keep control of your business.

As a business owner, knowing your numbers is absolutely vital. Quickbooks helps you to keep control of your business, and understand these numbers better than ever before.

With the information in this book, you'll have Quickbooks seamlessly helping you to run your business in no time!

Once again, thanks for taking the time to read this book, I hope you find it to be helpful!

Chapter 1
What is Quickbooks and is it Right for Your Business?

When it comes to keeping track of your company's finances, the accounting role is crucial. If you have never done any kind of accounting before, this can seem daunting at first. There is no need to worry, however, as there are many programs out there that are simple to use and are relatively inexpensive. The best of which is Quickbooks, which is the topic of this book!

Quickbooks, developed by Intuit, is software for your computer. It is specifically geared toward accounting and is great for small business owners who do not know much about accounting. This program is great because it is quite easy to use and it will handle almost everything you need in the way of basic accounting. It can generate invoices, handle payroll, credit card payments to you, track inventory and much, much more.

There are a couple of versions of Quickbooks. There is the basic version that will cover all of your basic accounting needs. If you want to add things like inventory and credit card processing, you will need to upgrade. On the basic level, it allows you to closely track money coming in and going out of the company. It also will keep track of who you owe and how much. Quickbooks is also great when it comes time to file your taxes because everything you need to calculate your tax payments is organized there.

Quickbooks combines everything you will need to create spreadsheets, balance sheets, cash flows, budgets, projections and everything in between. It is very user friendly and the primary function of Quickbooks is to consolidate all of your accounting needs into one system. Everything you will need is categorized and available when you need it with just one click. There is a lot to the program, but once you get used to the software and are familiar with where everything is, it will be a breeze!

When deciding whether or not this is the software for your company, you should ask yourself a couple of questions. Do you wish that accounting would just be a function that could perform itself, leaving you to deal with other functionalities of your business? Do you dream (or, in this instance, have nightmares) about numbers and invoices? Are you dreading tax time? If you answered yes to any of these questions, then Quickbooks is definitely the software for you. There are other options out there that are slightly less expensive, but their functionality pales in comparison to Quickbooks. Seriously, this is one of the best things to happen to small businesses!

Because you are going to be handling all of your own accounting, this book is going to cover the most basic, yet very necessary, functions in Quickbooks.

Most smaller businesses can get away with using Quickbooks Pro, which is approximately $169.00 which honestly, is quite a steal!

So, if you have not purchased the software, get to it! This guide is going to help get you through all of the functionalities you will be using, and will turn your accounting nightmares into a dream come true!

Chapter 2
Different Versions of Quickbooks

There are several different versions of Quickbooks, and different bundles of products that you can choose from.

Below is a list of the different offerings from Quickbooks for your perusal. Consider each option before choosing the best one for your business needs.

Quickbooks Online

Quickbooks Online is the online only version of Quickbooks. For this, all of your data is stored online on the cloud. There are three different pricing options for this available, starting at just $10 per month for the 'Simple Start' package, all the way up to $28 for the 'Plus' option which contains the most features. All options have a 30-day free trial so you really have nothing to lose!

Quickbooks Self-Employed

Quickbooks offers two self-employed options. They are the 'Self-Employed' option and the 'Self-Employed Tax Bundle'. The first is only $5 per month, with the Tax-Bundle option starting at $12 per month. These options are recommended for freelancers, contractors, and home-based entrepreneurs. Both packages are very similar, except the Tax-Bundle includes the TurboTax Home & Business program.

Quickbooks Desktop Pro

For a once-off price of $219.95 you can get access to the desktop version of Quickbooks Pro. In this version, all data is stored on your device. In includes all standard features of the Quickbooks program and will be enough for most small businesses. This version comes with a 60-day money back guarantee.

Quickbooks Desktop Premier

This version of Quickbooks costs $379.95 as a once-off payment, or $299.95 per year on an ongoing subscription model. It includes everything that the pro version does, except it also includes industry-specific features such as the ability to track your balance sheet by class, and bill clients progressively based on the job phase. This version comes with a 60-day money back guarantee.

Quickbooks Desktop Enterprise

This version of Quickbooks starts at $84 per month, and contains the most features. With this version, you can set up to 30 users, manage all of your accounting remotely, and add up to 1-million names so you can track hundreds of thousands of customers, vendors, and items. This version of best suited to the larger business, or those with a large range of products, vendors, and customers.

Quickbooks Mac Desktop

This version of Quickbooks has three different options. The cheapest is 'Simple Start' which begins at $15 per month. Next, you have the 'Essentials' package which is $30 per month, and finally the 'Plus' version which is $40 per month. All options offer a free 30-day trial. Each version offers a couple of additional features than the previous, such as being able to manage and pay bills, instantly create sales and profit reports, track inventory, and prepare and print 1099s.

Obviously, these versions of the program are designed to be used only on the Mac Desktop.

Hosting

All online versions of the program can be used on either a Mac or a PC. However, there is the additional cost of cloud hosting involved. You can find your own host for this, or for an additional fee, Quickbooks will host your data for you. The price varies depending on the package, and you need to call Quickbooks to get a personalized quote. If you select an online version, you can access your Quickbooks account from anywhere using a variety of devices, including through their app on both Apple and Android devices.

Chapter 3
Five Basic Functions of Quickbooks

Quickbooks has an incredible number of functions, but to start off simply, we are going to discuss the five most basic functions in Quickbooks. They are what most small businesses need to take care of their own accounting, and what you will likely be using the most.

1. **Vendors.** This is going to be the tab or function you see at the top left corner in your Quickbooks program. This is generally used to enter and pay bills within the vendor center. There are other functions within the vendor tab and they include; receiving inventory, purchase orders, and the ability to enter bills against inventory. Entering bills against inventory can be quite time consuming however, so keep that in mind.

2. **Customers.** Next to the 'vendors' tab, you will see customers. This is the absolute best place for accounts receivable or the A/R function. For the most part, almost all of the functions within the customer tab are useful. Take some time to familiarize yourself with this function and find all of the great things it can do for you. A little later in this book, we will discuss the functions in greater detail. For now, we are just outlining them so that you have an idea as to what we will be looking at in this book.

3. **Employees.** If you choose to do your own payroll (remember that outsourcing to a company like Paychex is always an option), this function is going to be where you will go to enter all of their time put in. This will help you keep track of hours and is great for knowing if

you are paying out too much in overtime, or if you need to hire additional help based on hours worked.

4. **Company.** The function here is set up for Chart of Accounts. Keeping this function clean and updated will make your month end duties to close out the books much easier.

5. **Banking.** This functionality within Quickbooks is super. There are shortcut keys so that you can write checks (ALT + W), a check register so you can monitor banking activities, and there is a function to print checks or bills.

Now that we have covered the basic functions of what Quickbooks will be able to do for you, let's go over what the majority of users consider to be the top Quickbooks features.

One of the favorite things among users is the ability to send invoices straight from Quickbooks to a customer's email. What is great about this function is you can also send out an invoice with two balances. If a customer has an unpaid previous balance as well as a new balance, Quickbooks can show that on the invoice so that it is clear cut and easy for the customer to read. Not only does this function save you the time and hassle of going to the post office, it also saves on stamps. Obviously, if you prefer to send emails via postal services, that is entirely acceptable as well. When it comes to accounting, it does pay to save yourself some time and energy however, and this functionality is great for that.

The second thing people love about Quickbooks is the forms interface. This is a simple to use, streamlined approach to your registers and journals function within Quickbooks.

Third, if you have the unfortunate pleasure of dealing with a customer who has not paid their invoice, Quickbooks actually has a function for that as well. In conjunction with Microsoft word, you will be able to send out a collection letter that is content appropriate, straight to your customer's email...just like the invoice.

Next up is the batch invoice function. This alone will save you hours of work. The information is input into Quickbooks and with one click of a button, your invoices will be sent to the appropriate customers.

In addition to all of the above listed handy features, Quickbooks can import and export from Excel spreadsheets for outside data storage. You can download a smaller version to your smartphone and check some of the most basic functions while you are out on the go or at a meeting. Quickbooks also has a backup function that will save your data automatically. You can also tell it what data to save and when. Setting that up from the beginning will save you a lot of time and hassle as well!

Now that we have talked about Quickbooks and explained the primary features and benefits, let's get into the nitty gritty and break down exactly how you will use the major functions within the program to perform the accounting duties for your small business.

Chapter 4
Completing the Easy Step Interview

Once you have installed your Quickbooks software, there is one step you will not want to skip and that is the easy step interview. This is an important part of properly installing and using Quickbooks. It does not take much time to complete and doing so will ensure your program is running as it should.

The first thing you are going to do is click on the *new company* link under the file tab. From there, you will click on *start interview* and answer all of the questions provided. Next, you are going to enter your company information. The only item that is absolutely necessary in this step is to enter your company name. However, all pertinent information you can put into the system will be helpful. Getting it done now will save you time when using the program later, and will make it run more smoothly.

Once you have answered all of the interview questions, you will be prompted to select the industry. This is an important step because based on the industry you choose, Quickbooks will actually customize the settings within the program to better accommodate your business and its needs.

Next you will tell Quickbooks how your company is organized by selecting your organization type. This is how you set up your company when you formed it either with an LLC (Limited Liability Corporation), C-Corporation, Sole Proprietorship or an S-Corp. This is also a key step in the interview process because it will help you with the tax filing portion later on down the line.

After you have set up your organization, you will tell Quickbooks what you want the first month of your fiscal year to be. This is entirely up to you. You can start with the beginning of the next month, January, or as most companies prefer, October. For a new business, it is suggested you use January, but the choice is yours.

The next step is to set up your administrator password. It seems like this would be done in the beginning, but Quickbooks thinks it is more important to get some other information out of the way first. If you are the only person using Quickbooks, make the password something only you would know, yet easy to remember. If there are going to be others using this program, the administrator password will allow only you to have unrestricted access to everything within Quickbooks. Other users can create accounts that will only all them to see the areas you (as the administrator) allow.

Finally, after you have set up the administrator password, you will be prompted to click 'next' and save Quickbooks to a location of your choosing.

Your program is officially set up, but there are many more questions to answer as part of the easy interview. There is going to be a series of questions for you to continue to answer until you come to the point where Quickbooks prompts you to finish. Because the questions are very specific to your industry, we will not go over what they are in detail here. Do not worry, though. Answering those questions will be one of the easiest things you do within the Quickbooks program. Once you are done with that, it will be time to move on to the next section.

Chapter 5
Setting up your Chart of Accounts List

There is a series of master lists you will need to set up in order to properly run your Quickbooks program. One of the first things we will look at is the Chart of Accounts list. Before we get into this entirely, it is important to note that you do not have to fill out each of these lists entirely. Get in as much information as you can in the beginning and add more customers or accounts as time goes on. This is one of the places within Quickbooks where you can actually leave information to be input at a later date and it will not affect the overall functionality of the program.

The Chart of Accounts List is one that will be used to separate and categorize your expenses, assets, income, liabilities, and the owner's equity. This area will house quite a bit of information. For example, if you want to budget by line item, you will need to create an account for that budget amount. The good news is, creating these new accounts is pretty simple and we are going to go step by step through setting one up now.

1. **Select lists then Chart of Accounts.** When you select this from the menu, Quickbooks will show the Chart of Accounts window as shown below.

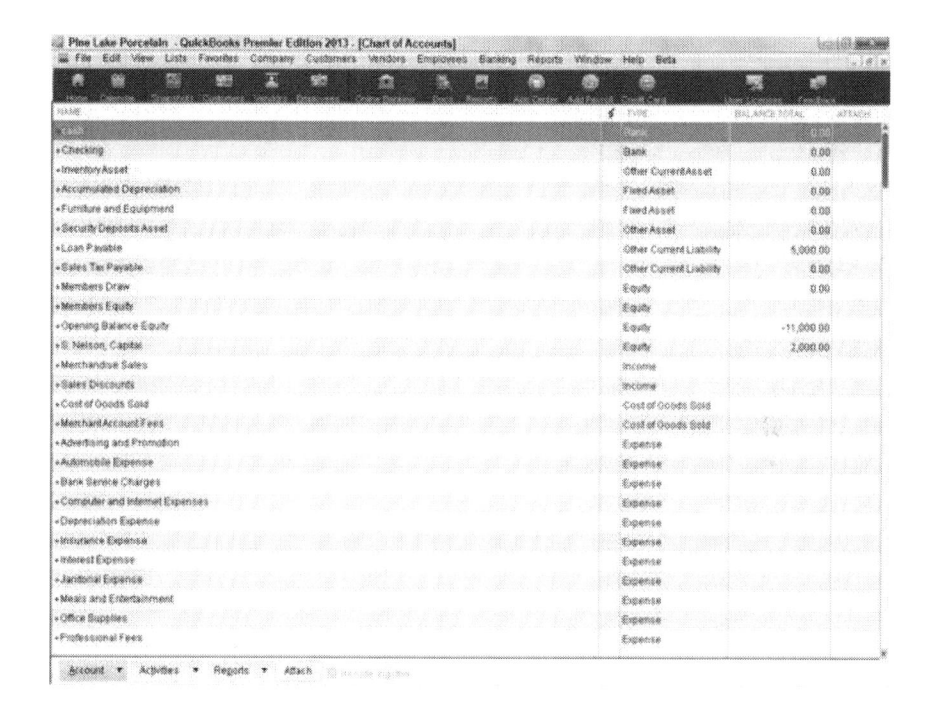

2. **Click Account at the bottom of the window.** This can also be seen on the bottom, left hand corner of the image shown above from step 1. From here, you will see the display from the account menu. One of the options here is *new* and that is the command you will want to use when adding a new account.

3. **Add the new account by selecting the *new* command.** From here, Quickbooks will show the new account dialog box, which is shown below.

15

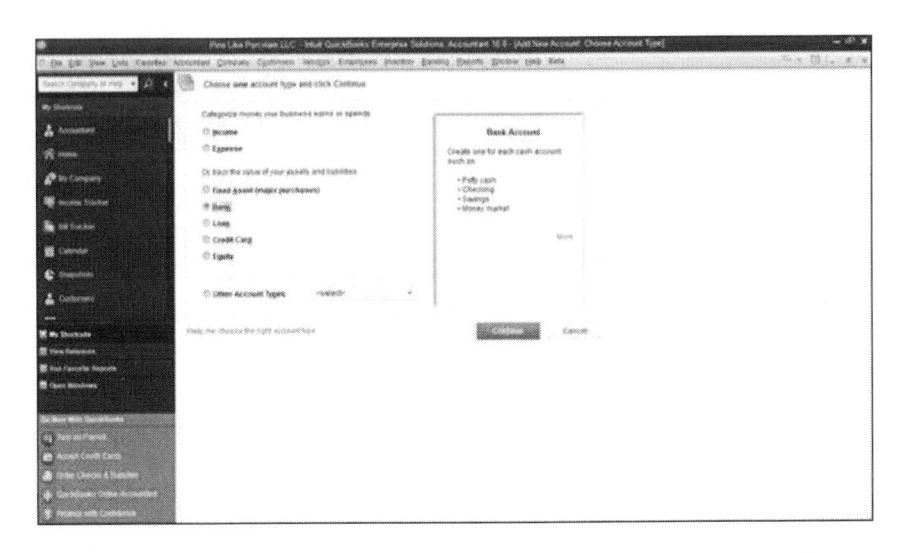

4. **Use Type button to select the account type to be added.** There is a lengthy list of account types to choose from here and you will want to select the one that that is best suited for your business need. The dialog box shows examples of the types of accounts you can select from. This is going to be setup to your company's personal specifications, so choose account types that make the most sense to you and your business.

5. **Click Continue.**

6. **Select a name.** When the new name box pops up, you will want to give the account a name that is going to show up on all of your financial statements. Make it something that will make sense to you and anyone using the program.

7. **Subaccount option.** If the account you've added needs a subaccount, you will select that option here. Selecting the subaccount will identify the parent account within Quickbooks.

8. **This step is OPTIONAL.** Provide a description of the new account. There does not need to be any description and Quickbooks does not need one to function properly. This is simply for you to use for your own purposes should you choose to do so.

9. **Other account information.** This is where you will provide other pertinent information for the particular account you have just created. An example of this is a credit card or bank account.

10. **Identify the tax line.** This might not be a necessary step if the data will not be reported on the company's tax return. Anything you will be reporting to the IRS will go into this subcategory.

11. **Another optional subcategory.** Here, you might want to consider an opening balance line for the account. However, this can be dangerous. Usually, you would not provide this information, but there is an additional new account box that will allow you to do so. This is not something I would suggest a new business owner do. Since it is an option, it is being mentioned. Accountants tend to handle this type of information, so leave it to the professionals. And if you are choosing not to hire one, avoid entering the subcategory for opening balances.

These eleven steps will help you set up the Chart of Accounts list. From this list, however, there is one more thing we can mention. There is an *activities* button that can be seen at the bottom of the window. This will display commands that will allow you to write checks, enter credit card charges, make deposits and journal entries, perform bank reconciliations, transfer funds and use the register. There is also a reports function that will display the commands that can be used to print all reports with account information.

Chapter 6
Setting up the Item List

The item list is incredibly important. This list helps you to keep track of what you have purchased, what your company holds in the way of assets and what you sell to the customer. In this chapter, we will go over how to look at your item list, using the item list, adding items to the list, and making edits to the items in the list.

In looking at the Item List, you will see that there are several different ways in which the information is stored within the Item List. If you have worked with Quickbooks already, you may be familiar with some of this while some of it may be entirely new to you. Either way, these next few paragraphs are going to detail the ways you will be able to see the items on the Item List.

First, let's take a look at the Item Column. This column is the one that you will see in many windows in Quickbooks. It allows you to view a drop-down list of things within the Item List. In this instance, you would use the Item column and then the individual rows within the Item column to properly identify those items appearing on an invoice.

An important note to make here is that while you look at the Item column, you will see that the drop-down box is quite narrow. If your item description is lengthy, a good portion of it will be cut-off. This may seem like a trivial bit of information, but you will want to remember it when you begin working with the item file. Here, you will want to use descriptive item codes, yet brief descriptions whenever possible.

Next, we are going to take a look at the Item List window. In order to get to this place, you will choose Lists, then item list, and Quickbooks will display the chosen item in the list window. This window will help you identify the item name or code, its description, and what type of item it is. You will also see the account that will get credit when you sell items from that list as well as inventory pricing and stocking information if that information was something you supplied. Below, you will see an example of the item list window within Quickbooks. Item lists will differ depending on how they are set up and what items you have in stock for your business. This is just a general idea of what you will be looking at with the Item List.

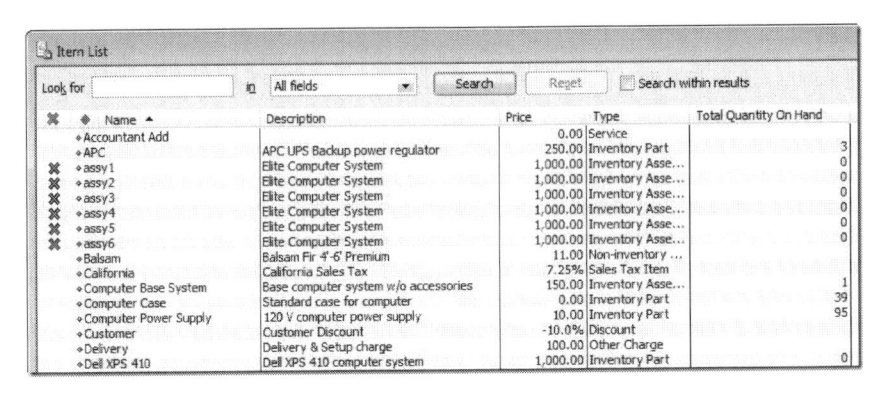

Name	Description	Price	Type	Total Quantity On Hand
Accountant Add		0.00	Service	
APC	APC UPS Backup power regulator	250.00	Inventory Part	3
assy1	Elite Computer System	1,000.00	Inventory Asse...	0
assy2	Elite Computer System	1,000.00	Inventory Asse...	0
assy3	Elite Computer System	1,000.00	Inventory Asse...	0
assy4	Elite Computer System	1,000.00	Inventory Asse...	0
assy5	Elite Computer System	1,000.00	Inventory Asse...	0
assy6	Elite Computer System	1,000.00	Inventory Asse...	0
Balsam	Balsam Fir 4'-6' Premium	11.00	Non-inventory ...	
California	California Sales Tax	7.25%	Sales Tax Item	
Computer Base System	Base computer system w/o accessories	150.00	Inventory Asse...	1
Computer Case	Standard case for computer	0.00	Inventory Part	39
Computer Power Supply	120 V computer power supply	10.00	Inventory Part	95
Customer	Customer Discount	-10.0%	Discount	
Delivery	Delivery & Setup charge	100.00	Other Charge	
Dell XPS 410	Dell XPS 410 computer system	1,000.00	Inventory Part	0

If you want more information about an item, you can always double-click it. By doing this, Quickbooks will display the Edit Item window. This function will show all the information you have about any given item. You can also use the Edit Item window to make changes to any portion of the item information you choose.

There are five basic steps to adding an item to your Item List. Items can be described in many different ways. For example, you would describe an item from inventory differently than that of the sales tax you would be required to charge. Because there is so much disparity in the way you will need to add descriptions to this Item List, we are going to just use the five basic steps to add an item. As you grow familiar with Quickbooks, you can add as you see fit.

1. **Click Lists, then, Item List.**

2. **Click the Item button on the lower left corner of the window.**

3. **Select New Command.**

4. **Use the various boxes for the new item window in order to describe the item you are adding.**

5. **Save.**

Next, we will briefly cover how to add certain types of items. Again, as all businesses are different, there is no way to cover each possible item in its entirety. For all intents and purposes, we will use generalization to give you an idea of how to set up certain types of items in your Item List.

One of the general items we might add into the Item list is a service item. This can be anything used to purchase or bill for items that are representative of a service. With your business, you are likely to have service items. For example, retailers and contractors will actually provide a service. Retailers may offer to gift wrap an item at an extra charge so that you do not have to. Contractors provide services like landscaping or painting. There are many types of services and Quickbooks will help keep these organized for you.

In order to add a service item, you will select the New Item window. From there, you will select service from the drop-down list type. This is where you will use that Item Name and

Number box to provide a service code or name. After that, you will select a subcontractor, partner, or owner and will indicate what services were performed by the subcontractor, partner, or owner. You will want to make sure this is clearly defined because each of those parties are subject to different kinds of tax rules. Finally, you will use the description box to give a brief description of the service. This description will appear on purchase orders and invoices, so you will want to use terms that are professional. You will then use the tax code box to determine whether or not the services provided were taxable. As a last step, you will use the account box to properly identify what income account will be credited when an item is sold.

Another item we will walk through adding is one for inventory. Items for inventory are those that will appear on purchase orders and invoices. They are representative of the physical goods you have bought, you hold in inventory, and that you will eventually sell. An example of this is retailers that have items sitting on their shelves have inventory that will one day be sold. Manufacturer inventory would be the raw materials that are purchased and then later used to assemble the products that are representative of that inventory.

To add an inventory part, you will need to display the New Item window. Once that pops up, select Inventory Part. Here, you will use the Item Name and Number box to give the descriptive, yet brief code and/or name for your item. From there, the Purchase Information and Sales Information box will allow you to determine the information that will appear on invoices and purchase orders. Again, be careful when entering this information as it will be visible to customers on the purchase order or invoice. Once you have all of your information added, you can continue to add until you have all of your inventory set up.

Because there are many things that can be added, we will move on. But, before we do, it is prudent to mention items that require sales tax. If you are going to sell items that are subject to tax, you will want to use Quickbooks to set that up as well. To create this item, you will click the New Item window and from there select Sales Tax Item from the drop-down menu. Once that is selected, Quickbooks will display the Sales Tax version. Here, you will use the Tax Name box to give an abbreviation of the sales tax. You can use the Description box to give it a full sales tax description. Finally, you will use the Tax Rate box to properly identify which sales tax rate to apply. You will then use the Tax Agency box to identify which tax agency you will be paying.

Chapter 7
Setting Up the Payroll Item List

In this chapter, we will cover Payroll Item lists within Quickbooks. This list will identify a number of items that will appear on an employee's payroll check stub. If you have decided to use an outside company to handle your payroll, you will not need to set this up. However, if your company is not yet in a position to be able to afford an outside service for payroll, or you wish to handle it yourselves, this chapter will go over the steps of getting this item list set up in Quickbooks.

Once you have your Payroll Item List set up, it will make your payroll day each week a breeze. When adding the payroll items, you will follow the steps outlined below.

1. **Select Lists then the Payroll Item command.** From here, Quickbooks will display the window for you.

2. **Add a new Payroll item.** Here, you will click the Payroll Item command and then choose New from the item menu. Quickbooks will display the Add New Payroll dialog box. From there, you can set up a new payroll item by using the EZ Set Up Method or you can choose the Custom Set Up Method. If you think you will need some assistance, choose the EZ set up method. Quickbooks will guide you through the process. Once you have selected the EZ setup, click next and Quickbooks will take you through the rest. If you choose to do this manually, you will click the Custom Set Up function and then click next. Here, Quickbooks will still guide you through the process,

but it is not as in depth as the EZ setup is. You will answer a variety of questions and then click next.

3. **Name the item for the Payroll List.** No matter which method you chose from the previous step, you will identify the type of payroll item here by naming it. Quickbooks will open a new dialog box that will allow you to fill in the information for each payroll item.

4. **Finishing the Payroll setup.** Once you have given the payroll item its name, you will click next to move through the remaining payroll setup questions. After you have identified the name of the government agency that the liability will be paid to, you will then enter the taxpayer identification number that will uniquely identify you to the tax agency. This is a number that would have been provided to you upon starting up your business. Once you have supplied all of the necessary information, click finish and Quickbooks will add the payroll item to your list.

This menu will supply the commands that will be useful for working with your Payroll Item list. Additionally, the commands you use when adding items to the list will supply more commands in the instance an item needs to be deleted from your payroll list. You can also rename any payroll item using this function. Finally, you can make payroll items active and print the list of all payroll items within Quickbooks.

Chapter 8
Setting up Your Customer List

In this chapter, we will cover the eight steps for setting up your customer list. The Customer List helps to keep track of all the customers you have as well as all of their pertinent information. The Customer List will track addresses, phone numbers, shipping addresses, etc. Follow the steps below to get your Customer List set up in Quickbooks.

1. **Select Customers, then Customer Center.** At this juncture, Quickbooks will display your Customer Center window and an example of this can be seen below.

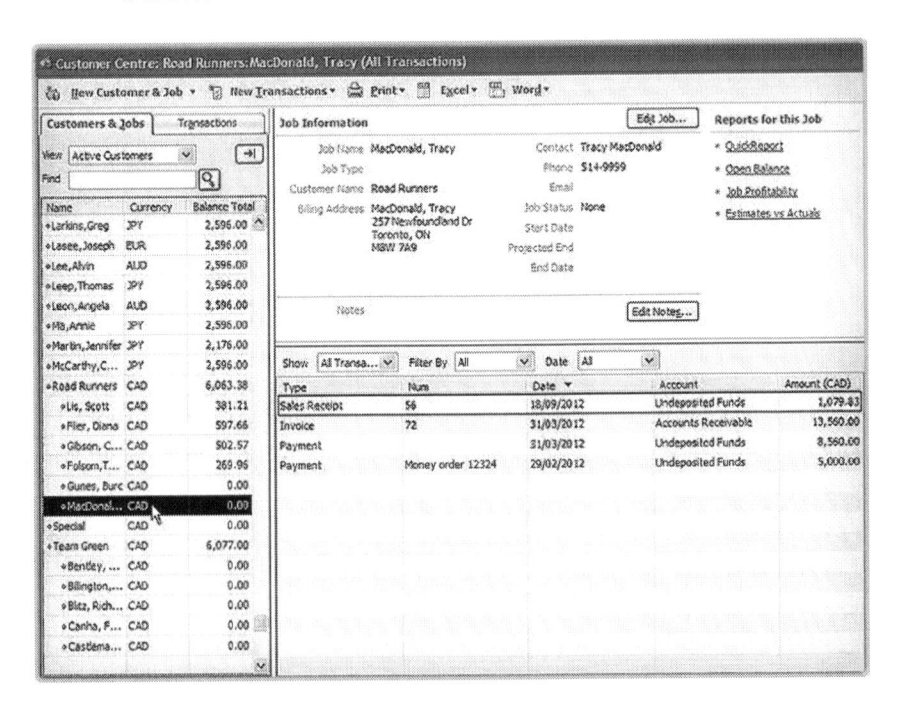

2. **Click New Customer and Job, then select the New Customer Command.**

3. **Give the customer a name.** It is not necessary to enter the customer's full name here. A shortened version of the name is easiest.

4. **Opening balances.** As mentioned in the chapter on setting up your accounts, this is one of those things most people will ignore. It is an incredibly detailed functionality of Quickbooks, which is great, but not necessarily for new business owners. In general, most users do not add opening balances mostly for the sake of their own sanity. Unless you have worked with Quickbooks extensively before and are familiar and comfortable with this accounting function, it is best to ignore it. We mention it for the sole purpose of order and that this is an option you will see when you are setting up a new customer.

5. **Address information.** Here you will enter all of the billing, shipping and contact information for the customer. You can include the contact name and phone number as well. However, just the information that pertains to the customer is good enough.

6. **Additional information.** This is not required, but it is a step in the process should you choose to use it. You can click a tab that is titled *Additional Info*. This is where you can store more in depth information about your customer. If what you provided in the previous step is good enough for you...great! Moving on.

7. **Click the payment information tab.** This will display a set of boxes where you will be able to record

customer account numbers, their credit limits if they have one, and their preferred payment method.

8. **Job Information Tab.** This is another optional step. It lets you give a detailed description of information associated with the job being performed for a customer. It is good for record keeping purposes and personally, I do recommend using it. Again, it is optional and if the information you have provided in the previous steps is sufficient for your bookkeeping purposes, then there is no need to enter anything else.

Chapter 9
Setting up the Vendor and Employee Lists

Because both vendors and employees are an integral part of any organization, we will briefly outline how to set them up in Quickbooks as well, before moving onto the banking functionality of Quickbooks.

Just as you will use the Customer List function to keep track of all your customers, you will use the Vendor List to keep track of all of your vendors. Like the Customer List, the Vendor List will allow you to record and collect information like the vendor address, who to contact, and so forth. We will first go through how to set up your vendor list, and then the Customer List.

1. **Select Vendor, then Vendor Center.**

2. **Click New Vendor button.**

3. **Name the vendor.** You will use whatever name you'd like in reference to your vendor within Quickbooks. Just as we mentioned with the Customer List, an abbreviation is acceptable with the Vendor List. Here, you will want to use something that is easy to enter and even easier to remember.

4. **Opening Balance and As Of fields.** This is one of those instances that I am mentioning the step because Quickbooks will prompt you to take a look at it. However, you will likely want to ignore this. As we have mentioned previously, anything to do with opening balances is going to be much too complicated

for the new user to Quickbooks. It really is unnecessary information for the owner as it is. Let accountants handle this, should you choose to hire them in the future. For now, it is a moot point.

5. **Vendor Address Information.** This tab is awesome. It has several easy to use and understand boxes that you can use to store your vendor name and other pertinent information. Here, you will want to enter the vendor's full name into the company name box. After that, you are able to click the address details tab that will prompt another dialog box to pop up. This is the edit address information box, which is where you will be able to enter the address in its legal format, which is the street address, city, state, and zip code.

6. **Additional information.** This is one of those, 'use it if you'd like' functions. Here, you can store any additional information under the Additional Info tab. When you click that tab, Quickbooks will show a dozen other boxes that you can utilize to store or collect information like vendor account numbers, payment terms for your vendor, what your personal credit limit is with that particular vendor, and the vendors tax identification number. You will definitely want to have the tax ID number stored for all of your vendors. When it is time for you to send the vendor the 1099 form, it will be nice to not have to go look for that information.

Next, we are going to cover how to set up your employees. It will be a little different than setting up vendors and customers, and somewhat similar to setting up payroll because the employee function in Quickbooks is geared toward paying them. There will be other information in there that is pertinent to the employee, but it is not an actual employee record that one would use for human resource files. This is all about accounting and doing things on your own within Quickbooks so here we go!

Within Quickbooks, you will see three options for setting up payment to employees. There is the do-it-yourself function, which is Standard Payroll. Next, there is the Enhanced Payroll and finally, Assisted Payroll. Because we are working on the assumption that you are performing all of the accounting needs for your own business, we are going to cover the Standard Payroll functionality of Quickbooks. As a tip and a side note here, if you are in a financial position to either pay extra to use Intuit Quickbooks Assisted Payroll or hire an outside service like ADP or Paychex, look into those options. They are equipped to fully handle the legalities and payroll taxes, deductions, and everything in between. If you are not quite there yet, that is okay because we are going to talk about getting your employees paid. Even if you are the only employee at this time!

Before you get into setting up your employees and getting them paid, you will need to do a web based interview for Quickbooks to get this started. Remember how we walked through that when you first set up Quickbooks? Good! That will make this next step simple. To go through the web based interview, you will click on Employees, then Payroll, then Order Payroll Service. From there, you will see the Payroll Setup page. Once you get to it, you will be walked through the interview process, and after it is complete, you will be ready to set up your employees.

Setting up your employees is pretty simple. You will select Employees, then Employee Center, and then click New Employee. Once you have selected the New Employee function, Quickbooks will pop up with a window for you to enter in all of the employee information. It will include their legal name, address, phone number and date of birth, social security, and gender information.

After you have described the employee for Quickbooks, you will go to the Payroll and Tax information section. This can be found on the Payroll and Compensation Info tab. Here, you will enter the payroll wages or salary into the earnings area. As an example, if your employee was hired at $30,000 per year, you would enter that in the annual salary box. You would then use the Pay Period drop down box in order to identify your pay period for the employee.

Next, you will need to describe what taxes an employee is to pay. From here, you will click the Taxes button. A dialog box will pop up prompting you to use the Federal tab in order to identify your employee's filing status, extra withholdings (if the employee specifies any), and the number of allowances they will claim. Basically, this is where they will file married or single, and list any dependents they have.

Because state taxes will vary from state to state, we will not be getting into the specifics here. Thankfully, Quickbooks has that all set up for you. All you need to do is click on the State tab which will prompt you to fill out a box describing the state taxes as specified by your state government. If your city has income tax information that needs to be entered, you can do that using the 'Other' tab function in Quickbooks. It will allow you to enter and store additional tax information as it pertains to your city or county.

There is a sick and vacation button that you can also use to pay your employees for this perk. What is really great about Quickbooks is that their tabs are clear cut and pretty self-explanatory. For instance, if you want to enter information regarding sick and vacation time, there is a tab that says Sick & Vacation. Within that box, you will be able to specify how much time is allotted per year and when an employee uses this time, you will be able to enter it to keep track of how much they have used and how much they have left.

Because so many people have moved toward using direct deposit, we will briefly mention it here. If you have chosen to use it, there is a Direct Deposit tab within the employee payroll section for you to click, even with the Standard Payroll service that comes with the simplest version of Quickbooks. Once you click the Direct Deposit link on the Payroll Info Tab, Quickbooks will prompt you to provide direct deposit information for your employee. I might suggest you set this up, even if it is only for yourself. That way, it is one less thing you have to worry about each week. Once it is set up, Quickbooks will handle the rest...we will cover that next!

In order to use Direct Deposit without having to manually enter the information every week, you can schedule what is referred to as a payroll run. This is a process that walks you through getting your payroll runs setup for however you plan to pay. Whether that is weekly, bi-weekly or monthly, the scheduling function will take all of the necessary information and run on its own from there.

Once you have set up the employee through the Standard Payroll function in Quickbooks, getting your employees paid is pretty easy. Go ahead and breathe a sigh of relief because this is great news! Below, we will outline the eight simple steps of getting your employees paid before we move onto the next topic.

1. **Select Employees, then Pay Employees, then Scheduled Payroll.**

2. **Start Scheduled Payroll.** In order to do this, you will click on the scheduled payroll that is shown in the box that will appear on the top of your Employee Center window. From there, you will select Start Scheduled Payroll.

3. **Check Date box.** Here, you will provide Quickbooks with the date you want to be shown at the top of the payroll check. This is done by identifying the date that the payroll period ends, which is provided in the Pay Period End box within Quickbooks.

4. **Identify Which Bank Account to write checks from.** Here, you will select which account you want payroll to come out of. If you only have one right now, that makes this process much easier. Regardless, always make sure you have enough money in the designated account to cover payroll.

5. **Verify Employees.** At this juncture, you will verify which employees are getting paid. Always double check to make sure this is correct. You would not want Quickbooks to cut a check for someone who left the company or took unpaid time off. However, if this happens you can void the check, which is also a pretty simple process. All you need to do is go to the Paycheck window choose Edit, then Void Paycheck.

6. **Click continue.** Once you have verified your employees, click continue. You can preview to make sure all information is correct. Once that is done, click the Create Paychecks tab.

7. **Print Paychecks or Pay Stubs.**

8. **Distribute Paychecks or stubs.** Depending on whether or not you allow for direct deposit, you will either distribute checks or stubs.

Now that we have talked about how to set up your vendors and employees to pay them, we will move on with how to set up invoices so you can get paid from your customers.

Chapter 10
How to Invoice Your Customers

In order to invoice a customer, you will need to use the Create Invoices tab to identify which customer is going to be billed and identify the amount they owe. To get to the Create Invoices tab, you will need to click on Customers, then Create Invoices. Once there, Quickbooks will have a display box for you to create your invoice. In this chapter, we will detail exactly how to invoice your customer.

1. **Identify customer and/or job.** In this step, you will want to identify the correct customer and/or job for which you are submitting an invoice. If this is for a customer you have not yet added into the Quickbooks system, you will be able to provide a brief description and other pertinent information for the customer in this screen so that you do not have to exit and go back to the customer screen in order to input the new one. Once you have completed your invoicing for the day, you can go back later and enter any new customer information in the Customer section.

2. **Confirm invoice.** Once you have identified your customer, or entered in the information for a new one, Quickbooks will automatically fill out the date, bill to, the invoice number, and in some instances the ship to address. If you entered the information correctly when you input the customer information, you should not need to change anything, simply verify the information on the invoice before moving on to the next step.

3. **Confirm invoice field information.** In this field you will see purchase order numbers, shipping dates, payment terms and the shipping method for this customer. You will want to make sure that Quickbooks has the information correct here.

4. **Description of items being sold.** How the invoice looks here will depend on whether you are selling services or products. With services, the column will look simpler because there is not as much information to provide. In the columns, you will want to describe each service or product. This will make sure that your records are kept neat and clean for later when you need to file taxes with the IRS. For each item or service, you will also enter the quantity and the list price. By entering the information in these fields, Quickbooks will be able to tally the total price to be billed for you.

5. **Customer messages.** This is a really great function within the invoices tab. There will be a footer at the bottom of the invoice where you can input in additional information or send a message to the customer. It can be something as simple as saying thank you for purchasing the product or provide additional information about the product for the customer. You can personalize each invoice for the individual customer, or make a blanket statement to use on every invoice.

6. **Check your spelling.** This is an optional step, but you will probably want to do this to make sure that your invoice looks as professional as possible. Quickbooks will do this for you if you select the Spelling button, which is at the top corner of the Create

Invoices tab. This function is much like the one found in Microsoft Word. It will highlight any incorrectly spelled words and give you choices for correcting them. On occasion, you might be using words that Quickbooks is not familiar with. If that is the case, you have the option to add it to the dictionary for future use.

7. **Save and close or save and new.** If you only have one invoice to enter, you can click save and close. If there are more invoices, you will want to click new so that you can continue to enter invoices. Studies show it is best to complete all invoices at the same time for many reasons, but the main being that you are billing your customers in a timely manner and that you are not forgetting to send an invoice. Customers are not going to call you to remind you that they have not been billed for a service or product they purchased. Well, most will not anyway.

There are a couple of other neat functionalities we will briefly touch on before moving to the next subject and that is either printing the invoice or emailing the invoice.

If you choose to print and mail an invoice you will click on the print button which can be found at the top of the Create Invoices screen. If you have several invoices to print, you can click the little arrow next to the Print button, which will give you the option to print a batch from a drop down menu. From there, you will Select Invoices to Print from the dialog box and click okay.

Emailing invoices saves paper and time. If your customer is okay with using a feature like this, it is strongly recommended. A lot of companies are moving toward this practice, so it is a good habit to get into from the very beginning.

In order to email an invoice, you will click the Send button and then Mail Invoice from the dialog box Quickbooks will display. When the Send Invoice dialog box is displayed, you can enter the email address for the customer and an email message should you choose to add that. Once you have entered the address and optional message, you will click the button that says Send Now and just like that, your invoice will be delivered to your customer.

Chapter 11
Budgeting Within Quickbooks

Being a small business owner, you are aware of the need to budget properly. After all, if you are unable to budget, you will not be successful and might not be able to expand, or possibly will go out of business. Using the budget function within Quickbooks is a great way to keep track of your business goals. Budgeting is how business owners and managers are able to plan out the operations for the year and decide what the financial goals will be for the upcoming year. Proper budgeting will help keep you on track and make sure that you are able to meet your financial goals.

That being said, there are a few ways you can budget. We will cover them briefly and then go over how to set up the budget function in Quickbooks. While there are countless ways to budget and manage your finances, we are going to cover the three most useful and most common budgeting techniques.

Top-Line Budgeting

The first is top-line budgeting. This is the simplest of the three because it takes the numbers from the previous year or month and uses them for the current year budget. If inflation occurred during the previous year, that is something that will be taken into consideration. On the other side of the coin, if the business shrank or came into some difficult times, previous year's or month's numbers will be decreased accordingly.

Zero-Based Budgeting

The next technique is called zero-based budgeting. This is the exact opposite of top-line budgeting. Zero-based budgeting will work from the bottom upward. It will start with revenue, then move up to expenses, assets, liabilities, and finally the owner equity accounts. The advantage of using this method is that it has the capability to fix previously budgeted amounts that were poorly figured. The new budgets are based on applications using common sense and simple math. This combination will quite often produce really great numbers.

Benchmarking

The final form of budgeting is known as benchmarking. This is an incredibly powerful, albeit less frequently used technique when it comes to budgeting. This will compare the preliminary or actual numbers budgeted to businesses that are of a similar size to yours. The challenge lies within finding comparable information for businesses that are like yours. However, with a little research and help from the local library or even industry associations, this information can usually be obtained easily enough.

In a moment, we will go through the steps of setting up your budget in Quickbooks. Before we get to that point, however, there needs to be a final thought on the three different types of budgets we have just discussed. As you probably know, it is not wise to use just one budgeting technique. While it may seem to work for a few years, this may become a form of complacency and you might find yourself in a financial predicament. When you use something consistently, you get to a point where you can pretty much perform those functions in your sleep. If you are not using your brain power to actually look at and analyze your budget on a regular basis, you can bet things will be missed. Use these three approaches in conjunction with one another, or use them once per year and rotate every third year. The point is, no one budgeting technique is fool proof or fail safe. Mix things up and keep that brain working actively on your budget!

Now that we have talked about the budget, let's go through the steps of setting up the function in Quickbooks.

1. **Choose Company, then Planning and Budgeting, then Set Up Budgets.** This is where you will input the amount you expect to receive for revenue and your expense accounting for every month during the year you are setting up your budget.

2. **Click Create New Budget.**

3. **Select the period or fiscal year.** At this juncture, a dialog box will appear and you will be able to choose which fiscal year you are working with.

4. **Select Profit and Loss.**

5. **Specify any additional profit/loss budgetary criteria then click next.**

6. **Choose budget from scratch or previous data.** If you are starting from scratch, select Create Budget from Scratch and enter your data. If you are using a previous year's data, you will select that option from the drop down box and click finish when you are done.

Those are the six, simple steps to creating a budget in Quickbooks. In closing, we will wrap up with a few comments on budgeting.

It is important to remember that while this may be a tedious task, it is crucial to your business' success. They are nothing to fear and it might help to look at budgets as something of a planning tool that will help you make sound decisions about the financial affairs of your business in the upcoming year.

If you are not finding value in budgeting, do not simply stop doing it. Find another method, and change it up like we discussed earlier. You do not want to let a budget go by the way side, especially when it is really easy to manage using the Quickbooks software. The trick is finding what drives the finances in your business. If it is sales, focus on that for budgets. If it is storage or manufacturing, make that the focal point of your budget. The point is, budget, budget, budget!

Chapter 12
Using Quickbooks for Taxes

As a business owner, filing taxes will be slightly different for your business as opposed to personal. There are many more deductions to look at and as a general rule, you will be paying taxes to the IRS quarterly. When it comes time to file your taxes for the entire year on April 15th, the hope is that you paid enough into taxes to not be socked with a huge bill at the end of the year. In all honesty, most small and even large businesses still have to pay taxes at the end of the year. However, the point of paying quarterly is to avoid sticker shock. Luckily, even if you did not plan as well as you would have liked, the IRS allows you to make payments. That is not the point of this chapter, though. Here, we are going to talk about how you can use Quickbooks and its sister program Intuit Turbo Tax to prepare and file your own taxes.

Quickbooks is going to be where you store all of your information throughout the year. Any sales tax, receipts for expenditures, purchases of equipment, rentals...anything you can deduct from your tax return. Quickbooks cannot actually transmit tax returns to the IRS, however and that is where TurboTax comes in. Because they are both created by the same company, Intuit, the two programs communicate easily with one another making filing your taxes a little less stressful.

The function of Quickbooks when it comes time to filing taxes is to prepare and then generate your quarter and year end reports. This will give an accurate portrayal of the income your business earned, payables, profit and loss, and much more. If you decide when it comes time to file your taxes that you would rather have a professional complete the task for you, Quickbooks will generate the report with everything the tax professional will need to complete your taxes. This makes the job for the CPA (certified public accountant) much easier and he or she will greatly appreciate the effort. If you are going to give filing your own taxes a whirl, Quickbooks will transmit the data to TurboTax into an easily imported format.

The first thing you are going to want to do is prepare your end of year reports. You will click Reports, then Profit and Loss, then Company and Financials. From there, you will select Last Fiscal Year from the Transaction Date drop down box and finally you will click Run Report. If you choose to view the report from the screen you can. You can also click Print to have a hard copy to look at while you are preparing your taxes for the IRS.

The next step is to locate Reports on the tool bar and click on it. After that, you will click Accountant and Taxes, then Choose Last Year in the Transaction Date drop box. You will then click on Run Report and finally Print to print your report.

Lastly, you will click Reports, then Vendors and Payables, and then 1099 summary. From there, you will click print to have a hard copy of your 1099 ready for tax purposes.

Now that you have all of that information, there are a few more steps to complete before you can either take the information to a tax professional or submit it through TurboTax.

Open Quickbooks and click on the File tab from the menu bar. From there, you will select Accounts Copy, followed by Save File.

After you have saved, you will click on Accountants Copy, and then you will click Next. From there, you will have the option to select the last day in the tax year (usually December 31st) in the Dividing Date box, then click Next. From there, you will click Save In from the drop box, and then go to the folder in which you are going to save the Accountants Copy for your backup to Quickbooks. For the file, you will want to use a descriptive name in the File Name field. It does not have to be excessively long or descriptive, but should contain enough information so that if you are looking for it, you will be able to find it easily. Something along the lines of 2016 taxes will probably suffice. However, name the file as you see fit and as something you will be able to locate when needed.

You now have everything you need to get your taxes completed and sent to the IRS. If at this juncture you decide you want to have an accountant prepare and send your taxes, you can download all of the information onto a flash drive and take it to your accountant. You can also email a copy if the accountant is in agreement to that method of tax transfer.

Alternatively, if you are going to use Intuit TurboTax (Business Edition) to prepare and then file your taxes, you will be able to import all of the data you just entered directly from Quickbooks to TurboTax. In order to do this, you will need to click on the Business Info tab in TurboTax, followed by the Quickbooks tab. From there, you will follow a series of prompts that will help you transmit the information from Quickbooks to TurboTax. Once the two systems have connected, you will click the Import tab, and the information will be transmitted from Quickbooks to TurboTax. This process will transfer the biggest chunk of your financial data. However, you will still need to go through the process of entering additional information. The system is very easy to use.

One thing to note here is that if you are planning to file your own business taxes by using TurboTax, you will need to make sure that the version of Quickbooks you are using has an activated registration code. If you do not, the information will not transmit from Quickbooks to TurboTax. You will also need to install TurboTax on the same computer that Quickbooks is installed on for this process to work.

Chapter 13
How to Create Reports

Creating reports regularly such as a profit & loss statement, or a balance sheet is key for any business.

Quickbooks makes this process quite simple, and these reports and many others can be created instantly at any time, for a variety of time periods.

To create a custom report, follow the steps below:

1. Click on the 'Reports' tab on the left hand navigation bar

2. Here, you can select from a range of reports such as profit & loss, balance sheet, financial ratio reports, and vendor expenses summaries. In this example, we'll select the 'profit & loss' option.

3. On the upper left-hand corner of the profit & loss report page, you can click on the 'customize' button.

4. Here, you can choose a custom time-period, choose your accounting method (cash or accrual), can add comparisons such as $ change or % change from a different time period, and can choose how much detail should be shown for each item.

5. You can then name the report however you'd like.

6. Click run the report in the bottom left-hand corner.

7. You can then save these customizations by clicking the 'Save Customizations' button at the top of the page. You can also export or email the report.

8. Finally, you can add the report to a group, such as 'Management Reports' so it will be stored there for viewing at any time.

9. To view your custom reports at any time, you need to click on the 'reports' tab on the left hand navigation of the home screen, and then click on the 'custom reports' tab.

This process can be followed for a range of different reports on all aspects of your business. They can all be saved in custom groups that you can create, and can all be exported, saved, or emailed instantly. Compared to the traditional method for manually compiling accounting reports, this feature makes accounting reports a breeze! Within minutes you can compare the performance of your business for the last month, to the exact same time last year, or against a variety of different time-periods!

Chapter 14
Quickbooks Add-Ons

There are several great Quickbooks add-ons that might be useful for your business. These are all compatible programs or services that integrate with Quickbooks to make running your business even easier!

This chapter will cover 10 of the best add-ons that you might want to consider.

AgileShip

AgileShip is a software that integrates with Quickbooks, helping you to find the cheapest shipping option. It draws order data from Quickbooks, and automatically compares shipping rates from U.S. mail, parcel, and freight services. It then selects the best option, and can set up the shipment by validating the address information, generating necessary documents, and records the cost into Quickbooks. AgileShip pays for the entire shipping process, and then invoices you all in a single consolidated bill.

Because this service pays the shipping companies up-front and handles a large number of orders, it gets volume discounts from shippers. Even after AgileShip takes its small cut, savings are still made by the customer. This service is definitely recommended if you're regularly shipping a range of different products to customers all over the country.

AuditMyBooks Analyzer

The AuditMyBooks Analyzer looks through your Quickbooks data, searching for suspicious or anomalous entries, helping to keep your staff honest, and also finding honest errors.

Starting at $8 per month, this service helps to protect you from fraud and errors. It sends you its results via simple reports.

SOS Inventory

SOS Inventory is a software that integrates with Quickbooks online to provide superior inventory management, order processing, and manufacturing support tools. It is completely accessible from all desktop or smartphone browsers. It includes the advanced features of support for inventory in multiple locations, and the ability to track items via a serial number. They offer a 30-day free trial. After that, it begins at $20 per month for a subscription that allows access by 3 users.

OneWay Commerce

OneWay Commerce allows you to easily turn Facebook into a sales channel for your business. It sets up a storefront on your Facebook fan page in a matter of minutes. The free version supports up to 9 different products and takes a 1.5% commission of receipts. The next version is $19 per month and supports up to 100 different products. All sales data is automatically integrated and tracked through Quickbooks.

Bill.Com

Bill.Com for Quickbooks online lets you receive e-bills (or store scanned paper bills) and pay vendors electronically, with transactions being automatically entered into your Quickbooks account.

This can save a lot of time that you would normally spend manually entering your bills and payments into the Quickbooks system.

It comes in at a price of $10 per month, plus $0.99 per payment. There is also an option available that integrates into the desktop version of Quickbooks.

Transaction Pro Importer

Transaction Pro Importer makes importing data from other applications into Quickbooks simple and pain-free. Normally, importing an Excel or CSV file into Quickbooks can be a headache. This web service does it for you, letting you edit and validate data before importing so that you can deal with any problems before they can affect your Quickbooks data. Subscriptions start at $20 per month.

Atduty Field Service

Atduty Field Service helps you to handle bookkeeping and management issues when you have remote workers. This web service has multiple features, including the ability to create schedules and work orders, tracking employees via a time card, generating invoices remotely, and accepting payments in the field.

This service has an Android app, and the pricing starts at $39 per month, allowing both Web and Mobile access.

OfficeAnt Customer Portal

This service generates a secure portal where customers can review and track orders, pay bills, submit support requests, and find answers in a knowledge base, forum, live chat, or FAQ section. If you can't always provide instant customer support, this portal service can be a huge time (and money) saver. You can customize your portal to include the features you want, and can design it in no time with the simple templates that they provide.

A free version supports up to 5 users, and paid versions start at $10 a month and provide support for up to 50 customers.

Postcard Services

Postcard Services caters for small businesses on a budget, who would like to reach customers via mail. For as little as $23 per 100 postcards, you can create a postcard from one of their many templates, and have it automatically printed and sent to the customer for you! It integrates with Quickbooks and makes use of the addresses stored on your Quickbooks account.

It also provides tools to track how successful your postcard campaign was.

Corelytics Financial Dashboard

This subscription-based web service analyzes the data from your Quickbooks account, and presents the results in easy to read charts and graphs. It shows how your business compares to others in the same industry, and can also be used to generate forecasts for future performance.

Chapter 15
Quickbooks Shortcuts

If you're going to be spending a lot of time using Quickbooks, then taking the time to learn the different keyboard shortcuts can make you a lot quicker at performing different functions.

This chapter will teach you the different keyboard shortcuts you can use to increase your efficiency when using Quickbooks. Keep in mind, that not all shortcuts may work for older versions of Quickbooks. If using a Mac, replace the 'Ctrl' key with the 'Command' key.

Transactions & Lists

- Ctrl-Del = Delete the selected line in a transaction
- Ctrl-Ins = Insert a blank detail line in a transaction
- Ctrl-N = Create a new transaction or list item
- Ctrl-D = Delete the current transaction or list item
- Ctrl-E = Edit an item list, or in a register
- Ctrl-O = If you are looking at a check in the 'write checks' window, use this function to copy the check. You can then use 'Ctrl-V' to paste the check.
- F5 = Refresh list

Opening Quickbooks Windows & Lists

- Ctrl-W = Opens the 'write check' window

- Ctrl-Q = Opens a 'quick report' for a list item when you have selected the item in the list

- Ctrl-Y = Opens a 'transaction journal' for a transaction, if you are viewing the transaction

- Ctrl-J = Opens the 'customer center'

- Ctrl-A = Opens the 'chart of accounts'

- Ctrl-I = Opens the 'create invoice' window

- Ctrl-L = Opens a list

- Ctrl-U = If you have just used Ctrl-L to open a list, this function will use that list item

- Ctrl-R = Opens the 'register' for the transaction you are looking at

- Ctrl-G = This will take you to the register for the 'transfer' account associated with the line that you have selected

- Ctrl-F = Opens the 'Find' window

- F1 = Opens the 'Help' window

- F2 = Displays the 'Product Information' window

- F3 = Opens the newer 'Search' feature or will open the 'Tech Help' window. This varies between versions of Quickbooks

- F4 = Opens 'Quickbooks technical support helper' window

- Ctrl-1 = Opens the 'Product Information' window

- Esc = Closes the current window

- Ctrl-F4 = Same as 'Esc'

- Ctrl-F6 = Moves to the next open window and makes it active

- Ctrl-Tab = Same as 'Ctrl-F6'

- Ctrl-H = Opens the 'Transaction History'

Maneuvering

- \+ = Increases the number in a form, such as a check or invoice number

- \- = Decreases a number in a form, such as a check or invoice number

- Alt-S = Saves the current transaction

- Alt-N = Saves the current transaction and moves to the next

- Alt-P = Goes to the previous transaction

- Tab = Go to the next field

- Shift-Tab = Go to the prior field

- Up Arrow = Go to the previous line in a form

- Down Arrow = Go to the next line in a form

- Page Up = Move to a previous page in a form area or report

- Page Down = Move to the next page in a form area or report

- Ctrl-Page Up = Move to the first item in a list or register

- Ctrl-Page Down = Move to the last item in a list or register

- Enter = If you are viewing a report, this will 'quick zoom' and open a register or detailed report. In other windows this will usually select the highlighted button/operation

- Ctrl-Enter = Record/Save the current record

Opening/Closing Quickbooks

- Ctrl = Starts Quickbooks without opening a file

- Alt = Starts Quickbooks without all of the windows

- Alt-F4 = Closes Quickbooks

Quickbooks Date Shortcuts

- \+ = Advances to the next day
- \- = Goes to previous day
- T = Today
- W = First day of the week
- K = Last day of the week
- M = First day of the month
- H = Last day of the month
- Y = First day of the year
- R = last day of the year
- [= Same day in previous week
-] = Same day in next week
- ; = Same date last month
- ' = Same date next month
- Alt-Down Arrow = Opens the calendar for date selection

Memorized Transactions

- Ctrl-M = Memorize the current transaction

- Ctrl-T = Create a new transaction from a memorized transaction

Miscellaneous Shortcuts

- Ctrl-P = Print

- Ctrl-R-P = If you have been trying to register Quickbooks and have been provided with a validation code, this will open the registration window where it asks for this code

Text Editing

- Ctrl-Z = Undo typing or any changes made in a field

- Ctrl-X = Cut selected text

- Ctrl-C = Copy selected text

- Ctrl-V = Paste text

- Del = Delete a character to the right

- Backspace = Delete a character to the left

- Home = Go to the first character in a field

- End = Go to the last character in a field

- Ctrl-Right Arrow = Move to next word in a current text field

- Ctrl-Left Arrow = Move to the previous word in a current text field

Chapter 16
Quickbooks Troubleshooting

As with any computer program, Quickbooks will have issues from time to time. This chapter will cover 10 of the most common issues that you will face when using Quickbooks, and how to easily resolve them.

Updating the Data File Fails

When you're upgrading from one version of Quickbooks to the next, a few issues can occur. Sometimes, the earlier version's data file can't be read by the updated version. To avoid this, make sure that you run a verification on the file before you uninstall Quickbooks or install the newer version.

Rebuilding the Data File Fails

Sometimes, verifying the data still won't upgrade it to the newer version. In this case, you'll need to go back to the old version of Quickbooks and rebuild your data. Do it in this order:

- Back up your data file

- Verify your data file

- Rebuild your data file

You Lose Connection to the Data File

This is one of the most common issues, and also one of the hardest to troubleshoot. This occurs if there is a hiccup in your network, causing you to lose the connection. A great tool to help fix this problem is the 'Quickbooks Connection Diagnostic Tool' as it will point you to exactly what has gone wrong in your network.

The Reinstall Fails

If you need to reinstall Quickbooks and it fails, you might not have done a clean uninstall of the program. To do this, uninstall the standard Windows uninstall method, but then go back and delete the C:\ProgramFile\Intuit|QuickbooksXXX Directory. Also, delete the C:\Windows/Users\DocumentsAndSettings\ProgramData\Intuit\QuickbooksXXX Directories.

This way, the program will be completely wiped from your system and will be ready for re-install. Remember to back up all of your data before doing this!

Quickbooks Runs Slowly in Multi-User Mode

There can be a range of causes of this problem, but if it's not your hardware acting up, it's likely to be being caused by issues in your data file. The fastest way to resolve this is by using the 'Clean Up Company Data' tool, found in File|Utilities.

Quickbooks Client Machine Can't Locate the Data File on the Server

To fix this, you'll want to first make sure that the 'Server Manager' is installed on the server machine, and that it's running.

You Can't Find the Licensing Information

If you've lost your documentation and can't find your license and product numbers, you can locate them by hitting either 'F2' or 'Ctrl-1' when Quickbooks is open.

A New Printer Won't Print

To fix this, you need to firstly, close Quickbooks. Next, search for the file 'qbprint.qbp'. Rename that file to 'qbprint.qbp.old'. When you restart Quickbooks, the printer should now work.

You've Lost the Admin Password

You can recover a lost password by using the 'Quickbooks Automated Password Reset Tool'. It's not 100%, but it does work the majority of the time.

You Can't Copy or Move the Quickbooks Data File

If you're trying to move a data file to back it up, sometimes the file will be 'locked' and won't move. To resolve this issue, close Quickbooks, click 'Start', 'Run' and then enter 'services.msc'.

Look for the Quickbooks services, and stop the 'Quickbooks Sever Manager' and the 'Directory Monitor'. Once they're stopped, you'll be able to copy & paste the data file.

Chapter 17
Final Thoughts on Quickbooks

We have covered a lot in this book and I hope you have found the information contained within it useful. First and foremost, I would like to reiterate how important it is to have a good accounting program to keep accurate books not only to make sure your business can continue to grow, but to ensure you have all the information necessary when it comes time for filing your taxes every year. There are so many great functionalities within Quickbooks that there is no reason your company shouldn't spend a little extra money to download the program if you haven't already.

If you have chosen to take accounting into your own hands as opposed to hiring a professional, Quickbooks will help ensure success. It truly is a vital program that, when used properly, will be able to make accounting much easier, especially if it is something you have never done before. Not only does Quickbooks provide you with great, simple journal entries, it gives you, the business owner, a sense of accomplishment. Handling the accounting for your small business gives you the power to truly know and understand every aspect of your growing business. You will find that this program is much easier than you expected and it will keep you abreast to everything related to the finances of your business.

Conclusion

Thanks again for taking the time to read through this book!

You should now have a good understanding of Quickbooks, and be able to comfortably use the program in your business.

If you enjoyed this book, please take the time to leave me a review on Amazon. I appreciate your honest feedback, and it really helps me to continue producing high quality books.

Printed in Great Britain
by Amazon